THIS BOOK BELONGS TO

....

....

Mom took Lottie and Benjy to the park for a picnic in the sun.
After eating their sandwiches, the children ran off to have some fun.
They were playing on the slide when they saw something they thought was bad:
A bully had stopped a tyke from using the swing—the child looked so sad.

Benjy and Lottie rushed over to ask the bully to stop being mean.
He told them to mind their own business, then continued to make a scene.
Lottie told Benjy to go get some help, so he ran as fast as he could.
He returned with their mom as the bully dragged the boy off the swing by his hood.

Mom told the bully's mom what her son had done to the other boy.
The bully's mom took him straight home and the tyke's sadness turned to joy
Lottie and Benjy invited their new friend to join them in their play.
They took turns pushing each other on the swing and enjoyed the rest of the day.

"It took real courage and strength to stand up against that which is wrong.
You performed a great act of kindness. You are both brave and strong."
Mom spoke with pride to Benjy and Lottie as they drove home that day.
"If bullies' actions aren't tackled early, they will never correct their ways."

Mom arranged a playdate for Benjy in the morning with his good friend, Jack.
Jack kept playing with Benjy's favorite truck and wouldn't give it back.
Benjy showed great patience as he waited for his friend to finish with the toy.
He wanted to play with the truck too, but was being a generous boy.

Mom had noticed Benjy's effort and, later on, she said,
"I know you love playing with your truck, but you shared it instead.
You showed generosity to your friend and lots of kindness too.
When I saw you being patient, I was very proud of you."

Lottie was struggling with her homework, an art project for school.
The collage was taking forever to finish and was not looking cool.
She was huffing and pacing the room when her brother came inside.
"What's up?" Benjy asked. "I'm struggling with my project," Lottie cried.

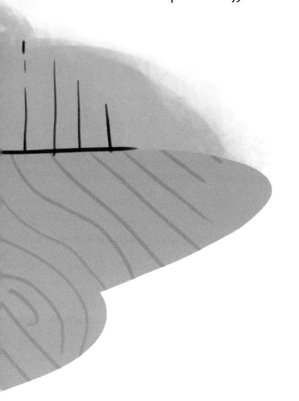

"Is that all?" he said. "Don't worry, I'll help. Just tell me what to do."

Lottie's face lit up as she handed him some paper and some glue.

"But you were playing," she said. "Are you sure you want to do this instead?"

"That's what brothers do. I'd rather help than see you sad," Benjy said.

As Lottie held up her masterpiece in front of Mom and Dad,
She beamed with pride at how good it looked. This made Benjy feel glad.
After Lottie left, Dad patted Benjy on the back and said, "Well done.
You showed real kindness to your sister. I'm proud of you, my son."

Benjy tried riding his bicycle without his training wheels.
He struggled not to topple as he yelled, "I hate how this feels!
I'll never be able to do it, I'm so bad at riding," he cried.
"I want to go as fast as Lottie when we go out for a ride."

"We all struggle with new things," Dad said. "None of us get things straight away. Be as kind to yourself as to others. Remember, Rome wasn't built in a day." Benjy kept trying. Soon, his parents cheered as he peddled with all his might. Although he was still a little wobbly, he managed to stay upright!

Thank you

What Did You Think of *Why Kindness Is A Strength?*

Thank you for purchasing this book. I know you could have picked any number of books to read, but you picked this book and for that I am extremely grateful.

If you like the book... and if you'd be willing to spare just two or three minutes...would you be willing to share your review of the book on Amazon?

If you would, it would mean the absolute world to me!

Thank you SO much. This helps to get the book into as many hands as possible, helping other parents and educators!

I really appreciate all your support!

Sarah Read
children's book author

Made in the USA
Middletown, DE
23 November 2020